Beginners Guide to Meditation
How to Start Meditating
An Easy, Practical Guide

Oliver Kent PhD

Dedicated to Ashley:

For sheer awesomeness and not killing me when I stole

your coffee.

Table of Contents

About the Author...xi
Introduction 1
Chapter 1 What is Meditation?.............................3
    Rituals...7
    Objects...8
    Repetition 9
    Anchoring...10
    Finding what works for you............................12
    Just 1 minute..13
    Get me out of here!.......................................14
    Find a safe place to put your mind 16
    Summary...18
Chapter 2 Awareness Meets Intention.................19
    Centering..20
    Peace..22
    Listening to the Answers................................24
    Finding Mushin...25
    Doing without thinking..................................26
    The Science behind it....................................29
    Let go of letting go.......................................29
        Trouble-shooting.....................................31
    The Divine..31
    Meditation of Loving Kindness......................33
    Summary...35
Chapter 3 Anytime, Anyplace, Anywhere............36

A different approach..................................39
The right tool for the right job...........................41
Making better choices...........................43
The Big Four................................44
Finding space............................47
The basic structure.............................48
Killing Time 50
    Example...........................51
Summary...........................52
Chapter 4 Seeing................................54
    Candles.............................54
        Troubleshooting...........................55
        Example...........................56
    Mandalas 56
        Example..............................57
    The Sky................................58
        Example..............................58
    Flowing water.............................59
        Example..............................60
    Doodling..............................61
        Example..............................62
    Summary..............................64
Chapter 5 Listening................................66
    Creating sounds..............................67
    Music and song..............................67
        Example..............................68
    Mantra..............................69
        Example..............................71
    Counting in base 2 or binary.............................72

Example..73
Singing Bowls.......................................74
    Example..75
Sleeping masks.....................................76
Summary..79
Chapter 6 Feeling and Doing.................80
3 breaths 81
    Example..84
    Troubleshooting....................................85
Childrens' games..................................86
    Example..88
    Rosaries...88
    Example..89
Finger knotting....................................90
    Example..90
Kata..91
    Example..92
Showers..93
    Example..94
Chakras 94
    Example..96
Incense...96
    Trouble-shooting..................................98
    Example..99
Summary..100
Chapter 7 Combinations........................102
Drumming..103
    Example..104
Crystals..105

Example..107
Mixing them together.....................................107
Example..107
Summary...108
Chapter 8 Now It's Your Turn............................110
Making it your own...112
Bringing meditation into your everyday life...113
Summary...118

About the Author

In his teens, Oliver had a conversation with a group of friends that profoundly changed his life. The first told of how awful his day had been. The second of how awful his week had been. The third went on to explain how awful his month had been!

And then they looked expectantly at Oliver...

"I'm actually having a good day" he replied.

This really wasn't a contest he wanted to win. The friend who'd been having a bad month promptly hugged him, hoping "Some of it would rub off."

While Oliver's not entirely convinced it works that way, he hopes that through his writing, some of his peace and happiness will indeed "rub off" onto the reader.

Introduction

"And so it begins..."

~Kosh Naranek

As a child, I once asked my father why he got up for work earlier than he needed to? I had a reasonable idea of how long it would take him to drive to work, and to me, the extra half an hour's sleep seemed like a much better idea!

He explained that he had two options. By getting up earlier, he left before rush hour. He drove down almost empty roads and when he arrived at work, there was plenty of parking. He arrived early at his office and spent the time enjoying the stillness.

So when work began, he was calm, refreshed and ready.

If he left later, he'd had to travel in rush hour. Then he'd have to try and find a parking space, possibly making himself late in the process. The whole journey would be stressful and he'd arrive at work tense and tired.

Put like that, it was a simple choice.

Sadly, daily life has gotten steadily more hectic. Back then, my father didn't have emails to contend with, or a mobile phone demanding his attention every five minutes.

No wonder that more of us look to meditation as a harbor from the storm. If we could just take some time and regain our sense of calm and inner peace... For many of us, things have gotten so bad, it's no longer about regaining it – we need to actually find it in the first place!

This book looks at the two main issues:

How do you meditate?

How do you find time to meditate?

Chapter 1 What is Meditation?

"The goal of meditation isn't to control your thoughts,
it's to stop letting them control you."

~ Anon

Nick wakes up to his alarm clock, swears, and mutters, "Just another five minutes..."

Half an hour later he wakes up, realizes the time and frantically gets dressed. He manages to wolf down a cup of strong coffee for breakfast and runs to the bus stop where he then has to wait around as the bus is late. Again. Anxiously, he checks his watch every thirty seconds, mentally re-calculating if he's going to make it to work on time?

The bus finally arrives and everyone surges forwards, each convinced that their need is the most important.

Nick manages to squeeze on and spends the journey alternating between mentally willing the bus driver to go faster and cursing the rush hour traffic.

When he finally arrives at his office, slightly late, totally out of breath and rather disheveled, he gets a disapproving look from his boss. He grabs another cup of coffee, sits down at his desk and starts wading through the mountain of pointless emails that magically appear each morning.

The day continues with fresh mayhem. People wanting things done with no notice and little explanation. Nick ends up skipping lunch and settling for yet another cup of coffee and a bar of chocolate from the vending machine.

Finally, even though the work-day comes to an end, it's another half an hour before he's able to leave. There's yet another horrendous bus journey, before grabbing some take-out. He opens a bottle of wine and sits down to watch tv shows, before finally crawling into bed.

But as he tries to go to sleep, thoughts run wild around his head, memories of all the day's injustices, the traffic, the ungrateful people... Soon the clock reads 3am and he's got to get up early again in the morning.

~

Nick's life isn't unusual. Despite advances in technology, it seems that the more "time-saving" things we accumulate, the less time we actually have.

Is meditation the answer? Wouldn't it be nice to pass untouched by the chaos? To somehow pass throughout our daily lives in a little bubble of calm? Most of us would settle for a decent five minutes of peace every now and then.

But what is meditation?

Simply put, it's a way of changing where you put your attention.

Often, like Nick, we have thoughts running through our heads distracting and worrying us. Instead of remaining trapped, rehearsing the same conversation over and over, meditation can break the cycle, allowing us to pause and refocus onto something more pleasant. Especially when we want to go to sleep.

It can also be used to bring our attention back into focus. When you're tired or bored and your mind is wandering all over the place, meditation can help you to concentrate on the important task you have at hand.

Fortunately, meditation is something you probably already do every day of your life without realizing it. Unfortunately, we tend to use it to distract us from life, often in destructive ways.

Replaying an argument you had earlier in the day, over and over again, is the same meditative technique as repeatedly reciting a prayer or poem. Likewise "Spacing out" and letting your mind drift from one random thought to the next, or working out your shopping list when you should be revising for finals, are both forms of meditation.

Just not usually helpful ones.

By making a shift to using meditation in a positive way and focusing your attention constructively, you'll start to see the benefits ripple out through your life. Being calmer, places less stresses on your body and makes you more resilient to those inevitable "moments" life throws at you.

Rather than having your attention pulled around like belligerent cat mauling a ball of wool, you get a say in what you want to think about. This in turn helps you see the bigger picture, rather than mentally shutting down and getting tunnel vision. It also lets you see the details, appreciating the beauty in everyday life that we so often miss a midst the rush and the hurry.

So how does meditation work?

While there are a lot of different ways to meditate, they tend to contain the same elements, just expressed in different ways. These are:

Rituals, Objects, Repetition and Anchoring.

Rituals

Human beings are good at noticing what works. Sometimes we find the answer because we were looking for it, other times the "Aha!" moment is a happy accident.

At the University where I worked, there a PhD student who was notorious for never cleaning up his equipment. One weekend, not only did he not clean up, he also left the furnace on by mistake! When someone opened the furnace on Monday morning, they discovered a brand new alloy which turned out to have properties that were potentially very valuable.

The problem – although they knew how long the furnace has been on and at what temperature, no-one knew quite what the starting concoction of his "left-overs" was, or how to work it out.

"Wait, you did what, with the who, now?" ~ *Barry Allen*

Often when people find a way of meditating that works for them, the first thing they do is to see if they can repeat it, creating a ritual in the process. If it works, after a while, some may tweak it a bit, but even then, that new version in turn, usually becomes a ritual. After all, it's much easier to do something you know is going to work, rather than to try and discover a completely new version each time you want to meditate.

Objects

Meditation often involves using objects. This can be anything from candles to bells to beads.

If you're going to use objects in your meditation, you may want to take time in choosing them. Rather than just using the first thing that comes to hand, explore and look for what resonates with you.

Much in the same way that children often have a favorite cup, teddy bear, or clothing, as grown-ups we can tap into this sense of wonder. That feeling of "rightness" in the objects we use.

Often the way in which the objects are stored is itself a ritual. Perhaps the bell is always placed back in the same place on a shelf, or the beads in a small wooden chest. Maybe the candles are wrapped up when not in use. Rather than just grabbing them and then shoving them in the nearest drawer when we're done, by taking them out and putting them away in a specific order you create part of the ritual to help "warm-up" for your meditation.

Repetition

In a similar way to rituals, once you've found something that works, it's much easier to keep repeating it over and over, than to come up with a longer version.

Longer versions are also much harder to remember.

The Christian rosary is heavily based on repetition. While holding a string of beads you recite the same prayer ten times. Each time, you advance one bead. This lets you focus on your meditation, rather than having to keep track of which number you're on.

After the tenth prayer, there's a gap in-between the beads to let you know to say a different prayer. This helps prevent your mind's natural inclination to get bored. Then you repeat the whole sequence again. The pace is left to the individual. I notice this in particular with Irish Catholics at hospitals - they get through their rosary prayers at breakneck speeds! But that's the pace that works best for them.

Anchoring

There's a neurolinguistic concept called "anchoring." Simply put, if you do something tactile, such as putting your hands together in a prayer gesture while you meditate, over time your mind will start to associate the action of placing your hands in that position with a meditative state, helping you get into it more easily.

This ties into all the other elements. By having a ritual, the anchoring effect gets stronger each time and in turn, will you'll find it easier to get into a meditative state. By using objects you add another tactile aspect to the meditation, allowing you to anchor to that as well, whether it's lighting the candle, or feeling the beads between your fingers.

Repetition also helps to speed up the anchoring process. Rather than just doing an action once each day, in some cases you may do it hundreds – for example when drumming – dramatically strengthening the anchoring effect.

An aspect of anchoring is choosing to meditate at a specific time, for a certain length. So how long should you meditate for and when?

There's a balancing act, much like Goldilocks and her porridge. Only instead of hot and cold, it's too easy or too hard. If the way you meditate is too easy, you'll get bored and your mind will wander off. But make it too difficult and you'll get frustrated and end up focusing on trying to do it, rather than actually meditating.

Like Goldilocks in her ideal, comfy bed, for meditation to work for you, it needs to be "just right". This can change over time. You may find when you're stressed and tired, that you need something much simpler and shorter.

There are times when you'll meditate for the length of a single breath – when you're in the middle of something and just need a moment to calm yourself, but simply can't stop for anything longer. And there are times you'll want to meditate for longer; if you've climbed a mountain in time for the sunrise, you may want to enjoy the view for hours.

It's not about fitting yourself into meditation, it's about getting meditation to fit into your life.

Finding what works for you

Imagine on your 18th birthday you were given a car and told it was yours, but it was the only car you'd ever be allowed to drive for your entire life. You'd probably take really good care of that car.

We know we only get the one body for this lifetime, yet we let our body, our mind and our emotions be run ragged.

If you've got a car, even though you know you can replace it, you're probably still careful not to drive around with the fuel tank showing just above empty. But too often that's what we do to ourselves, pushing to the point of exhaustion. Then we drink, or watch tv to distract ourselves, because the present moment seems too unpleasant to be in.

But when we think of meditation, it often conjures up images of monks sitting in a candlelit monastery or on top of a mountain in the Himalayas. It all seems to be very far away from our everyday lives. Even if we somehow do have a mountain nearby, most of us lead such busy lives, that even taking the time to drive up it and then meditate for just five minutes before driving back home, is probably time we don't have.

For many, just the idea of sitting still for five minutes isn't all that pleasant either.

Just 1 minute

The idea of meditating for thirty minutes can be daunting. In recent years, the 'Couch to 5K' program has looked at how best to help people who've never run, to be able to reach 5km. Rather notably is does not start with

"Go and run for 5km." Instead, the first week is a gentle walk to warm-up, then simply alternating jogging for a minute – slowing to a walk when needed - with walking for a minute. Gradually the times increase, until eventually, several months later, you find yourself running for a full 5k.

In the same way, you can begin learning to meditate with a brief warm-up - all you need to do is get comfortable. Then meditate for one minute. If you find yourself getting distracted, don't worry about it. Just go back to meditating when you feel ready. Then spend a minute being distracted. Wash, rinse, repeat. Over time, like the runners, you'll be able to meditate for longer periods.

Get me out of here!

"Today me will live in the moment. Unless it's unpleasant in which case me will eat a cookie." ~ Cookie Monster

It's all very well being told to "come into the present", but what if the present isn't a nice place to be? What if it's filled with stress, worry and pain?

"Watch your thoughts, they become words; watch your words, they become actions; watch your actions, they become habits; watch your habits, they become character; watch your character, for it becomes your destiny."

~ Frank Outlaw

If you look at the key words, "Words, Actions, Thoughts, Character, and Habits" their initials also spell "w, a, t, c, h."

Within Frank's advice is the power of meditation to change your life. Start by consistently changing your thoughts and the rest will follow in time. While the specific numbers vary, there's a general consensus that it takes about 21 days to create a habit and about 90 days to change a lifestyle.

Meditation is often initially approached as something separate from our daily lives. We "do" our meditation and then we get on with the rest of the day.

However, part of the beauty of meditation is that its effects are cumulative. Even little meditative moments throughout each day add up. This is one reason why meditating doesn't have to take hours.

There's a story of a King who offered Krishna any reward he wanted. First, Krishna asked for a chess board; he then explained that all he wanted was for the King to place one grain of rice on the first square, two on the second, four on the next and so on, doubling the amount each time. Krishna would then take all the rice on the board as his reward.

This seems like a remarkably modest request.

But if you do the math, that doubling effect adds up quickly - amazingly, you end up with about 21 billion tons of rice! In the same way, while a few seconds here and there doesn't seem like much, over time, it really starts to stack up and begin to change your life. Finding moments to meditate throughout your day, can be just as effective as spending a single hour meditating.

Find a safe place to put your mind

"If the words you spoke (or thought) appeared on your skin, would you still be beautiful?" - Auliq Ice

It's also important to ask yourself, where do you tend to put your mind? Especially when you're bored.

For example, when driving for long periods of time,

even if I listen to music, it can easily become "background noise" as thoughts wander around in my head.

The downside of Frank Outlaw's idea is that it also works for negative thoughts. If I habitually dwell on what's annoyed me recently, that's where I'll tend to put my mind. Something I've noticed is that for many people, they have a day that's 95% good and 5% bad. Let's say everyone was friendly to them, they got things accomplished, but then one driver cut them off in traffic and swore at them. That one ugly moment in an otherwise great day, will consume their mind. Take a moment and consider, where would you rather put your mind? Brooding in a foul mood, or smiling at all the everyday beauty around you?

The first step is simply becoming aware of where you tend to put your mind. Pay attention to what you think about during the day. Are you impacted more by the positive or the negative?

Then give some thought as to where you would like to put your mind? It can be practical – sometimes I'll think about the book I'm working on and how I can make it better. Or it can just be a more positive place – sometimes I like to focus on the beauty around me.

Over time, you'll find your habit has changed and you

now naturally put you mind in a better place. Which in turn impacts your words, your actions, your life.

Summary

- Meditation is a way of changing where you put your attention.

- You probably already meditate without realizing it.

- Meditating usually involves Rituals, Objects, Repetition and Anchoring.

- You need to find what works for you and your life.

- You can start with just One Minute.

- Changes add up over time and begin to improve your life.

- Find somewhere safe where you put your mind, rather than getting sucked into destructive thoughts.

Chapter 2 Awareness Meets Intention

"Quiet the mind, and the soul will speak."

~ Ma Jaya Sati Bhagavati

Usually during meditation, your awareness is moved to one of three places:

Peace

Listening to the Answers

The Divine

All three of these are aspects of seeking clarity. Whether it's finding your inner calm, clearing your mind and emotions so that you can actually see what's in front of you, or touching the Divine, it will work better if you start with a clear intention of what you want to focus on.

It's a completely free choice as to which you want to use. You may find you only prefer using one. This is fine; you don't have to do all three.

To move your awareness, you use intention.

Intention is simply making a conscious choice to do

something. Rather than letting your awareness drift around, you chose to focus on something specific. Intention is also what helps you keep your awareness where you want it, rather than being distracted by the noise of the children playing outside, or the shopping list you need to make for later on.

Take a moment and think about a Pink Elephant. You're now using your intention to think about that lovable creature, rather than something else.

Centering

Using your intention to focus your awareness on what you want to meditate on is called 'centering.'

Being 'centered' means that you've reached a meditative state of clarity. Centering is the process of getting to that point. With practice, you'll be able to become centered more easily and with deeper clarity. It will last longer, even after you've finished meditating and it will take more to un-center you.

In movies, the hero often reaches this centered state when they finally have their moment of clarity and understand whatever the lesson is they're supposed to learn. Their mind calms down and stops distracting them.

They finally feel like they can do whatever it is they need to. Luke becomes centered when he finally trusts the Force; Neo becomes centered when he finally believes he's the One.

Being centered won't let you break the laws of physics, but reaching this state tends to be why most people meditate. It's about finding a deep, inner clarity with which to meditate on Peace, Listening to the Answers or the Divine.

Although you'll hear people talk about "centering themselves", that tends to be a backwards description of what's going on.

You don't center yourself first and then use intention. You start meditating by using your intention to focus your awareness; this in turn, gradually centers you as you continue your meditation. It often happens in martial arts films - when the student is told to "center themselves" they use their intention – often closing their eyes, controlling their breathing and making hand gestures - shifting their awareness to start meditating, gradually centering themselves until they finally feel centered.

"Being centered" is a useful phrase to describe what you feel when meditation is working for you.

Also because the effect persists after meditation, it is possible to meditate to center yourself and then use that state of mind afterwards, for something practical. A surgeon may meditate to center themselves before surgery.

They may then use another quicker form of meditation - such as taking a few controlled breathes - if something disturbs them and they need to re-center themselves during the operation.

Peace

"Happy he stands, happy he sits, happy sleeps, and happy he comes and goes. Happy he speaks and happy he eats. This is the life of a man at peace." ~ Ashtavakra Gita

Let's begin by using our intention to move our awareness to meditating on Peace. Take a moment and see what springs to mind when you think about "Peace"?

There's no wrong answer.

Maybe it's a calm blue sky, or a still pond? Perhaps an empty house, or possibly a very full house filled with the people you love? Maybe it's the feeling of a mug of hot chocolate in your hands in the midst of winter? Or just a 'feeling.'

And as simple as that, you're meditating on Peace.

So why all the fuss – why rituals and repetitions and so forth? Well, people have found that without them, you tend to get more easily distracted by what's going on around you – mainly what happened in the past, what's happening right now and what you think might happen in the future. The argument with your sweetie, the children playing outside, or tomorrow's shopping list.

Sometimes it all gets so much, that after a while, you can barely even see, hear or feel your idea of Peace at all.

This is where all the meditation techniques come into play. In different ways, they help you use intention to move your attention to where you want it to go. By keeping it there, you'll be able to experience that sense of Peace more deeply; much in the same way that the longer you look at a work of art, the more you'll start seeing the subtler details that weren't obvious at first glance.

Listening to the Answers

The second common focus of meditation is Listening to the Answers - trying to solve the problems in our lives, from how to write a report, to which outfit to wear, or even world peace.

Throughout time, humans have puzzled over "Where does inspiration come from?" We know ideas and answers can sometimes pop into our heads, but how? The ancient Greeks believed that divine Muses would hand them out to the worthy.

In "How to Grow Rich", Napoleon Hill considers the monetary value of inspiration. After all, the Muses don't seem to demand any kind of tax or profit-sharing when you use their ideas and make money from them! You can take this idea further by going past just measuring it with money. After all, how do you put a dollar value on the inspiration of how best to communicate with your children, or the perfect present to get your beloved on Valentines Day?

But they're definitely valuable.

While we don't understand where inspiration comes from – and scientists are discovering that the idea of our brains just being organic computers doesn't explain a lot of things – meditating does seem to help the process of inspiration along.

Finding Mushin

"Meditation is all about the pursuit of nothingness. It's like the ultimate rest. It's better than the best sleep you've ever had. It's a quieting of the mind." ~ Hugh Jackman

The first part is Mushin - in order to hear the answers, first you have to actually listen. Mushin is a Japanese word that means "no-mind." It often likens your mind as being a pool of water, with your thoughts being ripples on surface, making it harder to see the bottom.

Mushin is the subtle combination of awareness without thoughts; your mind is completely quiet, allowing you to hear new Answers and inspirations. At first this seems like a paradox – how would you know if you weren't thinking? After all, surely you'd have to think in order to realize?

Take a deep breath in.

Your mind was probably quiet for the moment when you did that. Empty of thoughts. But you were still aware of what you were doing.

Popular metaphors for stray thoughts are a monkey chattering away in a tree, or a cat running around a room with a ball of yarn, merrily tangling everything up. Mushin stills them. You remain focused, but your mind becomes silent.

Doing without thinking

"Watchful, like men crossing a winter stream.

Alert, like men aware of danger.

Courteous, like visiting guests.

Yielding, like ice about to melt.

Simple, like uncarved blocks of wood." ~ Tao Te Ching.

One of the common mistakes about Mushin comes from variations of the following story. Two warriors have to fight, but the villain is more skilled than the hero. Someone teaches the hero that in order to win, he must attain Mushin, 'no mind.'

In The Last Samurai, Nobutada gives this advice to Tom Cruise's character, Nathan Algren, explaining that his focus is all over the place and his thoughts are distracting him from what's important - actually fighting.

"Hai. Mind the sword, mind the people watch, mind the enemy, too many mind... [pause] No mind."

Nathan takes his advice twice in the film and wins both times.

Sometimes the advice is phrased that the thoughts confusing the hero represent their own self-doubt and only by believing in themselves can they overcome the villain.

But there's a catch.

The hero usually overcomes his self-doubt at the end of the story after they've been become more skilled. In the film, Nathan spends months being trained in the art of sword-fighting by masters. When he's finally given the Mushin advice, he's reached the stage where he can sword-fight without needing to think about it.

If you've learned to drive or touch-type, it's the same thing. You just do it. You no longer have to think through how to change gear, or where "Y" is on the keyboard.

However, when we first start learning to do something we don't know how to do it. Gradually we improve and reach a stage where we can do it if we concentrate on it and can even recognize what's happening when it's going wrong. Eventually we can do it without needing to think; we've finally reached Mushin.

What Mushin won't do, is let you skip those stages.

I was driving one day at exam time, when the car in front of me suddenly stopped in the middle of the street. A rather flustered and clearly underage girl got out of the driver's side, while another older girl got out of the passenger's side and they swapped around!

It took me a moment to realize that the younger girl had been "trying driving" and had probably been able to cope on the quieter streets, but now she found herself in the middle of a town, things had gotten too much for her. Fortunately, both girls had the sense to swap, rather than carrying on until she crashed into something. But if she carried on learning to drive, then by now, she can probably drive through the same town while singing to the radio or chatting to her friend.

The Science behind it

Your brain has four "states", each named after a letter from the Greek alphabet. The alpha state is when you're relaxed – such as the moment when you've finally finished doing something and have a moment to yourself to just do nothing.

The beta state is the opposite – it when you're doing a lot of thinking, such as explaining to your Boss why you're late, but it really isn't your fault!

Delta state only occurs when you're in deep sleep.

The last one, theta state, is Mushin and it occurs when you're doing something without having to think about it –

showering, driving down a long empty highway and so on. This is the best state for Listening to the Answers. It also happens for about to fall asleep or wake up. You may have had the experience of being just about to drop off to sleep, or you've just woken up, and you suddenly got a moment of inspiration.

Let go of letting go

When you start to relax and clear your mind, thoughts will inevitably start to pop into it. This is your your subconscious sorting through all the clutter in your mind.

Most people's natural instinct is to try harder at not thinking, much in the same way the instinct when climbing a cliff is to hang on for dear life and as close to it as possible.

In both cases, though counter-intuitive, the better solution is to relax.

When meditating, see the thoughts, but don't interact with them. Let them wander around and gradually disappear on their own, a lot like watching clouds in the sky. There's no need to try staring or chanting them into submission.

One approach is to imagine your thoughts like a

waterfall. Let them just wash over you.

For the more IT-minded, the imagery of de-fragmenting your mental hard-drive can help. Just relax and let the thoughts flow past you as your subconscious re-orders them.

The amount of thoughts rattling around your subconscious is far more than your conscious mind can cope with. So even if you feel like your mind is full of thoughts, actually only a tiny number of them are there. The ones you're aware of are just passing through from your subconscious, and they'll eventually go back on their own; unless you focus on them and try to keep them in your mind.

Trouble-shooting

It's a good idea to have some way to record these ideas as they can fade and disappear as you leave the theta state of Mushin. A notebook or voice recorder both work well. Learning to write legibly with your eyes closed can help you get back into the theta meditative state more easily. (You may find that WRITING IN CAPITALS works better and *cursive* is harder.)

The Divine

"Meditation brings wisdom" ~ *Buddha*

People often worry that in order to meditate on the Divine, you have to be religious, or start following a different religion to your own. Fortunately, this isn't the case.

Scott Adams, writer of the Dilbert cartoon, has often been asked whether or not he plagiarizes from other writers' work. The question usually arises when the same joke or point was published in a cartoon, a day or two before his.

His answer is two-fold. First, when he plagiarizes, he does a much better job of hiding it! However, he then points out that cartoonists tend to look at similar sources for inspiration. Occasionally two of them will see the same thing and come up with the same joke or insight, completely independently.

In the same way, no-one owns meditation.

You'll see people of all religions and denominations praying by singing, from set prayers to hymns. And you'll also see workmen humming tunes to themselves as they work.

A Christian can use a Buddhist mala (string of beads, much like a rosary, but can be worn as a bracelet) to meditate, without being Buddhist.

A Hindu surgeon can meditate on simply clearing their mind before surgery, with no religious aspect at all.

In fact this happens quite a lot in religious services anyway. Many know the prayers so well, they can recite them without thinking and their minds drift off to meditating about the problem at work, or their shopping list...

You get to chose where you put your attention when you meditate. If you want to focus on Love, the Universe,

God, the Buddha, Thor or any other manifestation of the Divine, that's entirely your choice.

If you prefer to not to focus on the Divine, like the above surgeon, that's a perfectly valid choice too. And again, it doesn't matter if you're religious, agnostic, an atheist or something in-between – you get to make the decision every time you meditate.

Meditation of Loving Kindness

This is a traditional meditation based on blessing the universe with Loving Kindness. It's designed to be like a flower unfolding, or a ripple spreading outwards.

To begin: Relax, breathe, be.

Start by wishing yourself Loving Kindness. "Loving Kindness" is whatever works best for you. For some it's a golden light, for other's a feeling of warmth, or the actual emotional resonance of being loved. It may be an expression of the Divine, for example the blessing or love of a specific Deity, or something more abstract such as "The Universe", or even just "Love."

Then think of someone you like and wish them Loving Kindness.

These two steps are designed to build up a bit of

momentum, extending out Loving Kindness into the world. Gradually wish Loving Kindness to your town, city, country, the world and beyond until you're wishing Loving Kindness to everything.

Summary

- Usually during meditation, your awareness is moved to one of three places:

  Peace

  Listening to the Answers

  The Divine

- To move your awareness and keep it there, you use intention.

- Intention is simply making a conscious choice to do something.

- Centering is using your intention to focus your awareness on something you want to meditate on.

- Centering brings about a state of deeper clarity.

- Mushin is the emptying of your mind of thoughts.

- You don't need to be religious or change your religion to meditating on the Divine.

- The Meditation of Loving Kindness starts with loving yourself and then extending that Love across the universe.

Chapter 3 Anytime, Anyplace, Anywhere

"It's called a mala. Tibetan prayer beads.'
'What do you use 'em for?'
'I use 'em to calm my mind and to purify my thoughts.'
'Yeah, I use Jack Daniels!'
'See now, we're trying to go to same place. We're just using different technique.'
'Except I don't wear the bottle around my neck!'
'That's because you'd lose your job if you did...'
- The Glimmer Man

You may have seen the dramatic scene on TV or film where a character has just died and someone pulls out a syringe of adrenaline. They plunge it through the "dead" person's chest and into their heart, bringing them back to life.

This is how most people tend to think stimulants and alcohol work – they directly impact your body in different ways, such as relaxing or exciting you. A lot like pouring gasoline on a fire.

If that were true, meditation wouldn't help because it

doesn't add anything to your body.

The reality is a little different. Your body is capable of producing various chemicals, like Adrenalin. What normally happens is that under certain circumstances, your brain tells your body to release the appropriate chemical into your blood.

This chemical then causes your body to behave differently.

If you're frightened, it sends a message to release Adrenalin, making you feel energized and skittish. Whereas, if someone gives you a hug, a different message is sent, causing the release of dopamine and oxytocin, making you feel warm and happy.

Normally your brain does all this quietly in the background. You don't need to think, "Oh, I'm frightened" in order for your brain to do its thing. Similarly, you don't need to think about breathing or your heart beating for them to carry on – which is really fortunate when you're asleep! They work automatically.

However, like breathing and your heartbeat, you can choose to consciously alter them.

One way is to take stimulants or alcohol. Rather than behaving like gasoline on a fire, they "hot-wire" your body by faking their own messages, eg caffeine tells your body to release Adrenalin, even if your brain is calm and relaxed.

There's a couple of drawbacks to this. A lot of your body's automatic responses were designed to keep you alive back in the days of saber-tooth tigers. If you're being chased across the Savannah because "Kitty" thinks you'd make a good snack, Adrenalin is great for keeping you going. If while running you twist your ankle, Adrenalin will dull the pain and let you keep running; because if you escape, the ankle will eventually heal. But stopping and being eaten tends to be fatal.

"I'm learning to fly, but I ain't got wings. Coming down, is the hardest thing." ~ Tom Petty

But this system is designed on the assumption that this isn't an everyday event. After you've escaped from the tiger, then you get to rest and heal. The problem with drugs and stimulants is that you can make them an everyday event, knocking back triple espressos every hour while your body wonders why on earth it's reacting like being in a war-zone?!

One of the reasons that the drug Ecstasy is so dangerous, is that it allows you to "red-line" your body's

Adrenalin to the point of death. A friend told me of a patient brought into her hospital who'd suffered a heart attack from drinking too many energy drinks at once!

Similarly, the Vietnam war brought about wide-scale post-traumatic stress disorder, or PTSD, among war veterans. Prior to this, most wars were a bit more, well, orderly. Battles were usually fought at certain times. So there were points when you were up on Adrenalin, but there were also times where you were relatively safe and could relax. But in the Vietnam War, soldiers could be attacked at any time and this constant red-lining took a serious toll on the mental health of many veterans.

To add insult to injury, things that "hot-wire" your body often come with undesirable side-effects: alcohol and tobacco are poisonous.

A different approach

Another way is meditation. It's probably why you brought this book. So why meditation, rather than alcohol or caffeine?

A huge part of the answer lies in reconsidering what meditation is. If you view it as sitting alone in a room, chanting with incense for half an hour, then yes, drinking a glass of wine or smoking seem like a much easier, faster solution.

But if you broaden the options, things change.

I remember sitting an exam with about fifteen minutes left. Around me, people were either frantically writing, re-reading, or had given up.

I appeared to be asleep.

It was a practice exam and we'd been assured that the grade wouldn't affect anything, so I decided to use this opportunity to try different ways of approaching exams. For one exam I spent the night before cramming; for the next, took a 'day off' before the exam and didn't look at my notes at all.

While there's no universal "right" way to revise, - I know students who find success with both of those methods - I did discover something useful. We're taught to answer an exam and then immediately check what you're written. The problem with this is you tend to miss a lot of the mistakes – your brain auto-corrects as you read.

But if you take a couple of minutes to just close your eyes and think about something else entirely, it resets your mind and turns off the auto-correct, letting you see the mistakes.

For almost every exam I've taken since, I've taken a couple of minutes to meditate and clear my mind, before checking what I wrote and my grades improved because of it.

I could have gotten the same effect through taking drugs, smoking, or drinking alcohol – but there's two problems. The obvious one is that to the best of my knowledge, schools and universities frown on their students smoking and drinking in the middle of an exam! The other is that once you've "reset", you need to go back to concentrating. If you've just got drunk on tequila, you'll probably regret any "improvements" you make to your answers. (I've heard of an exam paper that was answered in the form of a long rant about why the student didn't need to know the subject. The markers were amused, but unable to award any grade.)

The right tool for the right job

I've also noticed that a lot of teachers embrace the rather bizarre idea that "being stressed before an exam is good."

Um, no. It really isn't. Being stressed releases Adrenalin which is only really good for fight or flight. So if you're planning on fleeing the exam and battering the door down, then ok, stress will help with that. But if you want to sit still at a desk for several hours and use your higher brain functions, not so much.

Again, this was one of the things I tried. I noticed that when we were waiting before an exam we'd all get each other stressed.

"Oh, I couldn't get to sleep at all last night."

"What if I get a bad mark, then I won't be able to..."

"Can you remember this obscure fact?"

and so on.

So for one of my practice exams I told my friends that this time, nothing personal, but I wasn't going to talk to anyone. I was just going to sit quietly, listen to the birds singing and enjoy the sunlight on my face. I went into the exam calm and relaxed with a clear head.

Again, my grades went up.

Driving is another example of where meditation helps a lot. The police tend to get grumpy if you drive while drunk, or on drugs. And while you definitely shouldn't close your eyes to meditate while zipping along the free-way, there are plenty of ways to meditate that don't impair your ability to drive and will help you be a calmer, more alert, responsible driver.

Making better choices

A common example is that someone cuts you up. Your body's fight or flight response will start to kick in with a release of Adrenalin, as your brain recognizes that this person could have injured or even killed you. The problem, is that if you go with "fight" you're now likely to go down a road that's actually more likely to get you injured. You honk your horn, swear, gesture and then chase after them, tailgating to prove your point. But in doing so, the risk of your being in an accident sky-rockets.

One of the strangest examples I've seen of this was a junction where the lanes were badly laid out. A taxi driver was in the correct lane. Another driver was in what seemed like the correct lane, but actually wasn't and so he needed to pull into the taxi's lane. Only the taxi driver wasn't having it. Due to the speed of traffic, they were both moving really slowly, maybe 5km/hr. I watched in amazement as they both tried to drive into the same lane together and gradually got stuck between the barriers on either side of the road.

They didn't even stop when they made contact with

each-other's car; they kept going until they were both firmly wedged in!

To add insult to injury, 100 yards further up that road is a junction with traffic lights. If either one had given way, they would both have been stopped at the red light and so it would have made no difference to their journey time at all. Instead, what they did probably cost them at least an hour, probably raised their car insurance and as it was in a capital city, almost certainly involved the police being involved.

Had they known how to quickly meditate while driving, it would have helped offset the Adrenalin spike and given them a moment of calm with which to make better decisions.

And let's face it, making a decision better than they did, isn't hard.

The Big Four

The main chemicals that your body produces to change your mood are Adrenalin, dopamine, oxytocin and cortisol.

Adrenalin is the fight/flight/fear response. It makes you faster, stronger and more tolerant to pain. Which is helpful if you're being attacked by a mountain lion. However it also tends to give you mental tunnel-vision. Do I stay and fight, stand still and hope it doesn't notice you, or run? It also tends to shut down your higher brain functions – the ones you use in trigonometry exams – as well as mess up your fine-motor skills, such as putting a key in a lock.

Stress, caffeine and other angry people tend to cause the release of Adrenalin, as does vigorous exercise.

With men, it tends to work faster and then wear off. But for women, Adrenalin tends to work slower and gradually build to a crescendo, taking much longer to wear off. There's also a huge spectrum of tolerance to Adrenalin. Those with a high tolerance need large jolts of it to feel its effects and so tend to jump out of perfectly good airplanes and go on roller-coasters in search of their 'aldrenalin high.' Those with a low tolerance can get spooked much more easily and tend to watch horror films from behind a chair while clinging to someone else!

So if you're a woman with a low tolerance to Adrenalin, having someone yelling at you can take ages for the effect to wear off, compared to a male 'Adrenalin junkie' who barely notices and quickly gets over it.

At the other end of the spectrum, you get a release of dopamine when you receive a reward. It's that feeling you get when you click "Buy" or you succeed at a task. Fortunately, this includes meditating. So even if you only meditate for a moment, you'll still get an increase in dopamine when you finish. When Listening to the Answers, you can get dopamine every time you receive a new inspiration.

Oxytocin is often associated with hugging. We mainly get it through touching and being touched. It's responsible for giving us warm and fuzzy feelings when people we like give us a hug. The main purpose of oxytocin is to help us bond to other people – it makes everyone involved seemed more friendly. Shaking hands with someone, or patting them on the back, will give you both an increase in oxytocin.

And lastly, cortisol is brought about by stress and wears you down, physically, mentally and emotionally. Fortunately, increasing your oxytocin helps to decrease cortisol. Increasing your dopamine helps to prevent cortisol from wearing you down.

Meditation can be used to help regulate these chemicals, giving you more control over your life. Meditating on Peace and the Divine, such as with the Meditation of Loving Kindness, can help you come down from the Adrenalin and cortisol that stress causes, while at the same time raising your dopamine and oxytocin, calming your body, emotions and mind.

Finding space

There's another way in which meditating is a lot like drinking alcohol: whether you do it openly and with other people?

Meditating alone and in private can require a bit of creativity – I know a surgeon who's found a large enough supply closet for him to meditate in-between surgeries to refresh and re-charge his focus.

Or you can hide in plain sight, the classic cup of coffee with a significant amount of whiskey in it! For meditation, one simple way of being left in peace in public is to pretend to talk to your phone. Act as if the other person is monologuing and just go "Uh huh" occasionally. The people around you will politely pretend that you're not there, letting you meditate in peace.

You can also meditate openly, though this depends a lot on where you are. Much in the same way if you put a bottle of whiskey on your desk at work, it might raise eyebrows, doing something that is obviously meditating may disturb the people around you.

Lastly, you can meditate with people who are doing the same thing. This is like going to a sports bar to drink with friends while you watch the game. Everyone's there for the same reason and drinking is actively encouraged! Religious ceremonies are a good example of a group of like-minded people gathering to meditate together.

The basic structure

"The bag's not for what I take, it's for what I find along the way." ~ MacGyver

While there are a lot of different ways to meditate, each one usually follows the same basic structure. First, decide if you want to have:

A specific time set aside for meditating. When and for how long?

A specific place. If so, are you going to enter and exit it in a particular way? Are you going to wear specific clothing, or sit in a certain way?

Are you going to do it alone or with others? Overtly or covertly?

Does it involve specific objects? If so, are you going to take them out and put them away in a certain ritual?

Next, choose your intention: Peace, Listening to the Answers or The Divine.

Decide on one or more ways to meditate from the rest of this book.

Meditate.

End your meditation in the ritual way that suits you.

Don't worry, although that seems like a lot of decisions to make, it can be remarkably simple.

~

Ben sets his alarm five minutes early. When it goes off, he wakes up but stays lying down comfortably in bed. He chooses the intention of Peace and goes through the Meditation of Loving Kindness.

Then he gets up and goes about his day.

~

There are many examples given throughout the book. We'll also revisit this structure at the end, after you've had a chance to choose some forms of meditation that you like and suit your life.

Killing Time

"All of life can be broken down into moments of transition or moments of revelation" ~ *J Michael Straczynski*

Modern life is a curious thing. We oscillate between having too much to do, needing caffeine to keep us afloat – and moments where there's nothing to do and boredom creeps towards us with its claws outstretched. Instead of reaching for a cross to deal with this particular vampire, often we reach for our phones or devices to ward it away with distractions.

Meditation offers us another way.

Rather than moments of "nothing to do" being a problem, they give us the opportunity to meditate and in doing so, build up our inner reserves, helping us better deal with whatever bedlam of the rest of the day may bring.

Example

Connor is waiting for the bus. And it's late.

Instead of reaching for his tablet, he takes a calming breath, focuses his intention on the Divine and mentally recites the Meditation of Loving Kindness in his mind until the bus finally arrives. This helps prevent him from getting frazzled by the aldrenalin and cortisol that would be released if he instead chose to marinate in his frustration at having to wait.

As he gets on the bus, he feels calm and refreshed. While the other passengers grumble at the bus driver for being late, Connor smiles at the bus driver in appreciation for doing a sometimes difficult job, recognizing that being late is most likely down to the traffic, not some deliberate attempt on the driver's part! In doing so, the bus driver receives some dopamine as he recognizes that he's valued; that will help him drive with a bit more care and patience, giving Connor a smoother ride.

Summary

- Your brain sends signals to your body to release chemicals that make it behave differently.

- This usually happens automatically, for example when you're scared.

- However, like breathing and your heartbeat, you can choose to consciously alter them.

- You can do this through meditation, stimulants or alcohol.

- Meditation is free, legal and can be done at any time.

- Making meditating a part of your everyday life will bring you more peace, as well as help you make better choices.

- Aldrenalin is the fear response.

- Dopamine is the reward response.

- Oxytocin is the hugging response.

- Cortisol is the stress response.

- Fit meditation into the spaces in your life.

Chapter 4 Seeing

"Looking at beauty in the world, is the first step of

purifying the mind."

~ Amit Ray

Throughout history, people have been inspired to meditate by the things they saw around them; from flickering candles to awe-inspiring sunsets.

Roughly half the people on the planet meditate by either thinking in pictures, or by looking at something. If this isn't you, feel free to skip ahead. Go to Chapter 5, 'Listening', if you prefer to meditate using sounds; or Chapter 6, "Feeling and Doing", if you want your meditation to be more physical.

There's no right or wrong answer, just do what works best for you.

Candles

Candles have long been used for meditation, religious ceremonies and relaxation. Flickering candlelight is surprisingly effective at creating a calm atmosphere.

There are several ways to approach meditating with candles. You can stare directly at the candle-flame; alternatively, look in the general direction of the candles. Or watch how the candle-light flickers on the surfaces of the room.

Try all three and see which works best for you. Again, there's a broad range of candles to chose from; different sizes, colors, scents and materials. By choosing one that you particularly like, you'll receive a 'reward' of dopamine every time you use it.

Troubleshooting

Obviously candles involve fire which is potentially dangerous - make sure there's enough ventilation and don't burn the building down! They also tend to drip wax, so either place them in a glass jar, or on some kind of dish that collects the melted wax, to protect whatever surface you place them on. You can also get candle holders, but be aware that with some designs, the wax can still run down the candle and then down the holder itself.

Example

During her lunch-break, Jill visits a nearby church and lights a small, votive candle. She kneels down and watches the soft flame, letting it bring her a sense of calm. She focuses her intention on the Divine and says a simple prayer to center herself, which reduces her cortisol and increases her dopamine. She then gets up and leaves, carrying on with her day.

Mandalas

If you ever played with a kaleidoscope as a child, you'll recognize the mandala pattern. They exist in an amazing variety of colors and core shapes.

In Buddhism and Hinduism, the mandala represents a spiritual map of the Universe. You can choose to use a specific mandala from one of those religions and the meanings that they've ascribed to it.

Or you can simply find one that appeals to you. If you have the skill and patience, you can create your own, though an easier alternative is to color in a line drawing of one to suit yourself.

Example

Bill buys a mandala coloring book. He searches through it until he finds one that he likes the look of and then spends an afternoon coloring it in a way that pleases him. He carefully cuts it out, takes it to work and places it in the center of the folder on Health and Safety procedures, content that no-one will ever look there!

Whenever he wants a quiet moment, he pulls out the Health and Safety folder, turns to the mandala and focuses his intention on Peace. He lets his eyes naturally move around the mandala, enjoying its beauty and the satisfaction that he helped make this and letting it center him, reducing his cortisol and aldrenalin, while giving him dopamine to counter the cortisol's effects.

After a minute, he closes the folder, replaces it receiving some more dopamine for having successfully meditated and goes on with his day, feeling refreshed.

The Sky

The sky really is the gift that keeps on giving. So often we get caught up in worries, or even our phones and forget to just look up. Each day it presents us with sunrises, clouds, lightning, sunsets, eclipses, the moon and stars. It's an amazing, ever-changing canvas that just needs us to look out of a window, or step outside. Failing that, even a picture can help capture some of its majesty, whether it's a calendar, photo, or background on your computer.

Example

Each day around sunset, Betsy goes outside and takes a photo of the sky with her phone. She then focuses her intention on the Divine, and simply stands there marveling at the beauty of nature. As she centers herself, she lowers any cortisol and aldrenalin she's accumulated throughout the day. When she's taken the photo, her dopamine increases making her feel happier and protecting her from any lingering effects of the cortisol.

During the day, whenever she needs a pick-me-up, she pulls out her phone focuses her intention on the Divine and scrolls thorough the pictures she's taken, raising her dopamine and re-connecting to the feeling of awe, again lowering her aldrenalin and cortisol.

Flowing water

Like the planet we live on, our bodies are mostly composed of water. So it's not surprising that many find it aids them in meditation to look upon moving water; whether rain, waterfalls, rivers, or the ocean. Each form plays with light in different ways, from the soft pitter-patter of spring rain on windows, the sweeping torrents of autumn storms across the sidewalk, to waves rolling back and forth as they crash against a beach.

Unlike most meditations, this one probably requires you to have access to something fairly significant – an ocean, river, or constant "bad" weather. It usually requires more preparation, especially the logistics involved. In some countries, rain and storms are a regular thing. In Ireland there's a joke - "If you can see the mountains in the distance, it's going to rain. If you can't see them, it's raining!"

Traveling to a nearby river or beach may require specific clothing, such as hiking boots, as well as a means of transport. You may also want something to sit on, such as a blanket. However, succeeding at getting there will give you dopamine. If going to actual water is impractical, there are a large number of videos freely available on YouTube you can use instead.

Whether you use real or digital water, look at the light playing in and across it, choose your intention and meditate.

Example

Brad lives in Seattle, where it can seem like it's always raining. When he has spare moments, he appreciates the rain, watching the drops steadily falling onto roofs and windows. When he finds himself waiting for a bus, he makes the choice not to spend that time getting frustrated, knowing it would just raise his cortisol and aldrenalin.

Instead, he focuses his intention on Peace, looking at the rain running down side of the bus shelter to center himself.

Doodling

While drawing takes a significant amount of skill, doodling is far more accessible. Like many of these forms of meditation, it's something we often naturally did as children, doodling away on our composition books. As grown-ups we may instead find ourselves doodling absentmindedly on post-it notes while we wait for a file to download, or on nearby pieces of paper when we're put "on hold."

Hearts, flowers, stars, houses and random squiggles are the more common doodles.

You can also use different colors. Look online, or go to an art store and buy some pens or pencils that appeal to you, both in color and also in the way they feel in your hand.

It's also important not to get caught up in judging the "quality" of your doodles. This isn't about drawing; quite the opposite, embrace a more childlike approach of accepting your doodles just the way they are.

Example

Kate is trying to write a report; but she needs to put across complicated concepts for readers with little or no knowledge of the subject. Every time she tries to start explaining something, she realizes for it to make sense, there's something else she needs to explain first! Kate can feel her cortisol levels rising as she gets increasingly stressed.

To break the vicious circle, she takes out a sheet of

paper from the office printer and picks up a pen. Kate focuses her intention on "Listening to the Answers" and starts writing ideas down on the page, occasionally doodling between them. She lets go of trying to "get it right" and instead waits for it to slowly unfold in front of her, as she becomes more centered, she feels her mind opening up and fresh insights start occurring to her.

Finally she has an "Aha!" moment and realizes that by changing the categories she was using, there's now a simple place to start. The accompanying reward of dopamine helps motivate her to begin re-organizing her report with this new approach.

Although she stops actively meditating at this point and starts working on her laptop, the state of being centered persists and she finds it easier to see where each piece of the report now fits into this new way of organising it.

Summary

- Candles – be wary of the fire hazards.

- Mandalas – find what suits you. You can create or color in your own.

- The Sky – works both with the 'real' and digital versions.

- Flowing Water – you may need to organize some logistics.

- Doodling – don't be distracted by judging the quality of your doodles.

Chapter 5 Listening

"The quieter you become the more you can hear."

~ *Anon*

Listening is a fundamental part of meditation across history and cultures. Science has recently discovered that different rhythms actually change the way your brain works.

Importantly, for some, sound has a more profound impact on them than movement or light. If you skipped the Seeing chapter and came straight here, hopefully this will be more in tune with you.

One of the most common occurrences of this is hearing music you listened to as a teenager. (If you're not a teenager yet, then know that the music you will listen to when you are, will be with you for the rest of your life – choose wisely!) It evokes memories and feelings of that time, whether listening to a break-up song, or something more motivational. It's a big part of the reason each generation tends to believe every other generations' music wasn't as good as theirs – they simply don't get the same resonance from it.

Creating sounds

"Listen to the sound of waves within you" ~ Rumi

When it comes to sound there are three main approaches:

You can listen to someone else,

Produce or imagine the sound yourself,

Or both.

Again there's no right answer, find what works best for you. You may even feel that you prefer different approaches when you're in different moods. You may find when you're exhausted, it's better to listen to someone else. Or you may find that making sounds reinvigorates you.

Music and song

Using music and song to meditate is as old as human

history. Thankfully, we live in a time with incredible access to instruments as well as recordings of every kind of music imaginable. If you're comfortable playing an instrument or singing, you can do that as you meditate; or record yourself first and then play it back.

Alternatively, use a recording from someone else.

Music and song naturally lend themselves to groups, from chanting and hymns at religious ceremonies, to singing along at rock concerts and raves. This in turn often involves oxytocin, whether it's shaking hands or bouncing up against each-other. Partner dancing is especially good for this.

Example

It's halfway through a concert of Emma's favorite band. The warm-up act did a great job and now everyone's standing on their feet, bopping around and gently bumping against each-other, having a great time. Emma brings her intention to the Divine through the abstract concept of Love. Love for the band, for her fellow revelers, for everyone! She sings along, letting the lyrics carry her on waves, spilling out Love to everyone around her as her oxytocin rises.

Mantra

There's a story of a traveling monk who meets a farmer. The farmer politely asks him if there's a way to meditate while farming? The monk teaches him a mantra – a short phrase – and tells the farmer to recite it to himself as he goes about his day. The farmer thanks him and the monk goes on his way. A few months later, the monk passes by the farm and asks the farmer how things are going? The farmer is delighted. The mantra has helped quieten his mind and gradually brought about a sense of inner peace to his daily life.

The farmer then happily recites the mantra.

And there's a catch. The mantra is in a language the farmer doesn't know and he'd slightly misheard it. What he's actually been reciting translates as

"Oh Holy Cow."

The monk nods, smiles and goes on his way without correcting the farmer. What's important is that the act of reciting it, combined with the rhythm and cadence of the words is giving the farmer peace. For the farmer, the actual meaning of the words isn't what's important.

Similarly, I've seen a cartoon of a father with his newborn baby perched on his lap. The father is reading the

71

sport section to his son, specifically the report of a boxing match that had gotten rather bloody. On seeing this his wife is rather alarmed, but the father points out that his son doesn't know what any of the words mean. As long as he says them in the same cadence as he'd read a bed-time story or nursery rhyme, what difference does it make?

It's important to use mantras with rhythms that resonate with you.

On the other hand, many dancers of Argentine Tango don't speak Spanish and so can't appreciate the poetry and meaning behind the words being sung to the music they dance to. For many, listening to opera is a similar experience, although hopefully the singer conveys some idea of the emotion being expressed through their body.

"Making teenagers depressed is like shooting fish in a barrel" - Bart Simpson

But if you do understand the words, it's important to consider the impact they have on you personally, especially emotionally. You may find you prefer different mantras, depending on which mood you're in.

To meditate with a mantra, first chose a word or series

of words. Decide if you want them to be relevant to what you want to meditate on eg "I wish love to all", or just words "One, two, three, four." Then decide if you want to say them out loud or in your mind.

Remember the Goldilocks aspect to find the sweet spot. Fine-tune it so you neither get bored or frustrated. Part of what makes mantras so useful is you can use the simpler ones anywhere. I find "And breathe..." is a particularly useful one when navigating crazed rush-hour traffic.

Start to repeat the word(s) over and over. Let the rhythm bring you into a meditative state. Bring your focus to what you want to meditate on. This may include the meaning of the words.

You may also find that closing your eyes and sitting still helps to block out visual and physical distractions.

Example

Sally is about to go onto the ice for the regional figure-skating competition. She's alone in the changing room. So far, she's gotten dressed using the same ritual she always does, left skate first, then right, both tied with a double knot. She sits on the wooden bench, closes her eyes to remove any distractions and focuses her intention on Peace, as she quietly repeats to herself

"I'm a leaf on the wind, watch how I soar."

When she feels peaceful and centered, her cortisol lowered and her aldrenalin under control, she repeats her mantra one last time, feels the fresh spark of dopamine as she opens her eyes, takes a deep breath and then gets up to go and compete!

Counting in base 2 or binary.

A surprising number of mathematically-minded people do this, without realizing that they're meditating.

Technically, the binary mantra should be something like "0, 1, 10, 11." In practice, most prefer to just keep constantly doubling the number:

"1, 2, 4, 8, 16, 32, 64, 128..."

and so on.

Example

Tom works in for an IT department and has returned to work after a week's holidays to find that *someone* has rearranged all the leads in his office and now nothing works. At first he looks at the spaghetti-like mess in front of him and is overwhelmed. Where does he even begin to start?! He feels his cortisol start to rise as his body begins to react to the stress.

He focuses his intention on Listening to the Answers and starts to count in Base 2. Each time he successfully recites the next doubled number, gives him a small reward of dopamine and helps to center him.

When Tom reaches 1,024 he's centered and his cortisol is back under control. He realizes that it doesn't matter where he starts. Like counting in Base 2, what's important is to start and take it one step at a time.

He sits down, unplugs the first lead and carefully starts untangling it from the others. Each time he finishes unraveling a wire, he's rewarded with a new boost of dopamine, helping him continue with the task.

Singing Bowls

You've probably seen a video of someone "playing" wine glasses. The idea is simple, fill them with different amounts of liquid; then wet your finger and trace around the rim to produce different notes depending on how full they are. Singing bowls are similar to this, but without the need for water.

To meditate, use the stick to make a stirring motion around the outside of the bowl. A continuous sound note will start to form, though it may take a few moments to get going. Don't grip the bowl tightly in your hand as it will stop the vibrations. Either rest it on your palm, or on another soft surface. You can also strike the bowl with the bamboo stick if you prefer a single chime

Bring your focus to what you want to meditate on.

Begin making the sounds you've chosen.

Example

Adam is half-way through his end-of-term paper. Each night at 7pm he sits down at his desk, opens the top drawer and takes out the brass singing bowl he discovered in a small shop, hidden in a dusty sidestreet, while on a visit to Nepal. Simply taking the bowl out and enjoying having it, increases his dopamine.

He brings his attention to Peace, picks up the wooden stick, gently strikes the bowl and traces the stick around the rim of the bowl. He brings his intention to Listening to the Answers and gradually feels the sound centering him.

After a few minutes, he feels centered and tuned into the subject of his paper. He stops, putting the bowl and stick back in the drawer and receives more dopamine for completing the meditation. Adam turns to his computer and starts to type.

Sleeping masks

While visual aspects like candles help some to

meditate, they're a distraction to others. Many prefer to meditate by closing their eyes.

It's a different experience closing your eyes when your surroundings are light, rather than dark.

One of the problems with modern life is, unless you live in a rural area, it rarely gets dark any more. Even at night, street-lights create an almost permanent dawn, which thoroughly confuses the songbirds where I live. Likewise, many of us have moved away from the old farming rhythms of going to sleep when it gets dark and getting up with the sun. We find ourselves trying to sleep while sunlight streams through the curtains.

As for trying to meditate during the day...

Fortunately sleeping masks block out ambient light, allowing you to meditate in "darkness", regardless of how well lit the area is.

One issue with sleeping masks is feeling pressure on your eyes. Some modern sleeping masks are designed to solve this by creating a space around your eyes. This removes the pressure entirely and even allows you to open your eyes. With this, you're able to experience meditating with your eyes open in complete darkness, whenever you want.

With this version of sleeping mask, there's enough space for your eyes that you can look around naturally. One of the unintended consequences of modern life is that we've gone from gazing around our surroundings, to spending a lot of time staring at screens. Even though you can't actually see anything while wearing these masks, letting your gaze wander around can be refreshing. It's especially useful if you spend a lot of time working on computers as it also gives your eyes a break from the glare of the screen.

Sleeping masks come in a variety of materials. The ones that allow you to open your eyes tend to be made from stiffer materials to hold the necessary shape. The more traditional ones that touch your eyes, come in a range of synthetic materials, as well as cotton and silk.

You may find that your skin is sensitive to some materials, or that you just prefer the feel of certain kinds. Fortunately most sleeping masks are fairly inexpensive, so it can be worth trying out a few to find what works best for you. I have a different one for my bedroom (simple silk) than I do for my work-desk (one where I can open my eyes.)

Everyone's face is slightly different, which means that

sleeping masks will often allow a certain amount of light in around your nose where the mask doesn't lie completely plush against your skin. It can also vary if you're lying on your side. Sleeping masks also come with a variety of different straps, from velcro which can get caught up in long hair, to adjustable straps which can be uncomfortable if the adjuster is where you want to rest your head.

Reading reviews can help, but it seems like a certain amount of trial and error, combined with luck, is the way forward.

Summary

- Music and song – you can use recordings or perform them live.

- Mantra – while the words don't have to matter, you may find it works on a deeper level for you if they relate to where you're moving your intention.

- Fine-tune the level of ease and complexity to suit how you feel.

- Counting in binary – just keep doubling the number

- Singing bowls – strike or stroke around the outside of the bowl.

- Closing your eyes and sitting still helps to block out visual and physical distractions.

- Sleeping Masks can help with this; find the type that suits you best.

Chapter 6 Feeling and Doing

"And it was King David - King David, who we read
about in Samuel - and what did David do?
What did David do?
*What **did** David do..?*
David danced before the Lord with all his might,
leaping and dancing before the Lord." ~ Footloose

One of the drawbacks of meditation is that it can seem too cerebral, and not really grounded in the physical reality that surrounds us.

Fortunately, there are a number of approaches that address this. Some focus on how your body moves. Others work with objects, paying attention to moving them and how they feel, rather than their appearance or sound.

Focusing on the physicality of these meditations and the feelings they invoke, has a strong anchoring effect, especially if you're someone for whom this approach to meditation is a good fit.

3 breaths

Often a reason for wanting to meditate is to help us deal with all the everyday "stuff" running around in our heads, messing about with our emotions.

One solution is to make this work for you.

Choose something you think about a lot. It might be a piece of work with an approaching deadline, or maybe a daunting presentation you have to give to a group of people, or even someone you've just broken up with.

Every time you think of it, you're going to try to take three breaths.

On the first breath, you're going to focus on something positive and abstract.

Hope, love, God; something like that. You don't need to be too precise. Just focus on the connecting with whatever it is for a moment and take a breath. A version I particularly like is the better version of me. The person I'd be when I'm older if I make good choices. Because that potential exists your entire life.

"To see infinity in a grain of sand and eternity in an hour" - William Blake

Next, you're going to connect to something you find awe-inspiring. Often this involves something that your mind can't really comprehend. The sky is "up there", but how far away is that? Likewise the stars seem to only be a few miles away, but the actual distances are incredible.

At the time of writing, your computer probably does something like 1,000,000,000 processes a second! Imagine trying to create a machine that works by magnetizing and de-magnetizing tiny sections of material, billions of times a second?!

Even simpler things have astonishing degrees of

complexity. Look at your clothes. How long would it take you to make them by hand? What if you had to create all the tools and material from scratch? Consider all that was involved to just make the right color dye.

There's a video on YouTube called "I, Pencil: The Movie." It's adapted from the 1958 essay by Leonard E. Read and looks into how amazing and complex the process involved in making a pencil is. No matter where you are, you'll always be surrounded by wonder.

Lastly, take one more breath to just settle yourself and get a bit more centered.

Then, if you want, think about whatever you were going to. The aim isn't to stop you worrying, or thinking about your ex-girlfriend. It's about slowly building up a second effect in your life to help balance it. Think of each meditative breath as a single rain-drop. On their own, they seem inconsequential, but over time, they can have a powerful effect.

This is partly due to an effect known as "brain gardening." During the day, whenever you think of something, your brain creates chemical markers that help you get back to that thought more easily. Conversely, the things you don't think about become harder to access. It's a lot like pathways in a forest. As long as they're frequently used, they stay clear. But if they fall into disuse, they become increasingly overgrown and hard to travel.

The thing that you're thinking about a lot today, will be different from the thing you're thinking about a lot next week, month or a year from now.

But the pathways in your brain that you use for this meditation will stay the same. Meditating regularly helps keep them clear and easy to access.

Example

Ashley has seen the most exquisite pair of boots that she absolutely must have!

When Pay-Day comes.

Eventually.

Until then, she finds her mind keeps drifting to day-dreaming of finally owning them and taking them out on the town.

Every time she finds them appearing in her mind, she mentally pauses for a moment and focuses her intention on Hope that the day will go well and takes a breath. On her next breath, she looks at the bracelet she's wearing and wonders at how old the gemstones set in it are?

Millions, even billions of years old? On her third breath she focuses her intention on centering herself.

And then she fantasizes about the boots!

Troubleshooting

The first problem you may run into is figuring out what to connect to for the first two breaths? This might take a bit of trial and error - take some time to play with different ideas.

However, even if you're stumped for now, just chose 'something' and do it anyway. That way, you'll have the habit of meditating like this already in place, when you find which 'something' is best for you.

Although it sounds strange, the second problem lies in actually taking three breaths at all!

If you're struggling with this, all you're going to do is to try to take a single breath. If you only end up taking half a breath, don't worry about it.

In your own time, work up to having just an in-breath for 'positive', and an out-breath for 'awe.' You'll find you naturally take another in-breath which you can use to settle yourself.

Eventually it will sort itself out. It might take days,

weeks or even months, but it doesn't actually matter. Just let your body and mind grow into it at their own speed and their own way. Much in the same way each tree grows upwards in a slightly different way, trust yourself.

Also, don't feel that the three breaths must all be the same, or last a certain length of time. Like the waves of the tide coming onto the beach, they don't have to be identical.

Relax. Trust.

Again, like the ocean waves, don't feel you have to strictly follow this. One day you might find you take a whole breath when focusing on the positive, and then just an in-breath for awe. On another day, you might find you take several breaths to settle yourself.

Each moment is different. Do what feels right for you.

Childrens' games

Childrens' games are a ready source of inspiration for meditation practices. Many forms of meditation are really just grown-up versions; we buy gemstones or statues, rather than collecting interesting pebbles from the beach, pine-cones from the forest or rocks from a trail.

Children's games often follow the framework of

meditation. There's usually a ritual of how things are supposed to be done 'properly', often with special objects. The intention is usually changed to having fun, which is a worthy thing in itself. But you can change the intention to one of the 'grown-up' three of Peace, Listening to the Answers and the Divine.

Marbles, yo-yos, jacks and paddle-balls all work well. More recent innovations include fidget spinners. Again find one or more that appeals to you.

Then decide on a specific ritual. Yo-yos and paddle-balls naturally lend themselves to creating a rhythm similar to drumming, whereas marbles and jacks are more about movement in space; but they all have a strong physical aspect.

Keep in mind Goldilocks' porridge. Walk the balance between keeping the complexity at a level that's neither boring nor frustrating.

Example

Amanda gets a fidget spinner from her secret Santa. She likes the feel of it in her hand and so starts using it to meditate.

During the day, whenever she starts to feel a bit

overloaded by people's demands, and her cortisol starts to rise, she takes a moment for herself and pulls the spinner out of her pocket. Just the feel of it in her hand causes her body to releases dopamine, as she enjoys that it's her's. She focuses her intention on Peace and spins it a few times, letting the feel of the vibrations sooth her, lowering her cortisol again.

Rosaries

From Catholic rosaries to Buddhist Malas, using a string of beads to meditate has been around for a long time. Again, at its heart, it's a rhythmic process, moving beads through your fingers.

Meditating this way is pretty easy to disguise, making it

ideal for everyday life and office work. You can use normal beaded jewelry and just look like you're fidgeting with it. Or you can place it on your lap and surreptitiously do it under a table.

To meditate, get your preferred string of beads. Decide which action you'll do for each bead – maybe a specific prayer, or a breath.

Bring your focus to what you want to meditate on.

Carry out the action that accompanies each bead, moving on to the next one when you've completed it.

Example

Katy is concerned about a presentation her son has to make later in the day. During a quiet moment, she takes out the rosary she received as a childhood gift from her aunt and chooses her intention as the Divine. She says a specific prayer to God each time she moves along the rosary, one bead at a time, asking for Him to help her son.

Finger knotting

The gesture of two hands clasped together in prayer is recognized across religions and cultures. In the west, crossing your fingers for good luck is also pretty common.

Buddhism makes use of this in the meditative practice of "knotting" your fingers. One of the simplest is simply making "rings." Place you thumb and first finger together and then link the rings they make.

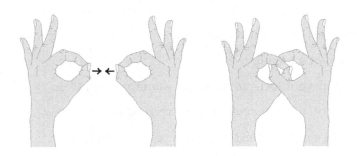

One of the benefits of this technique is that by using a different finger you potentially have four different anchors. So you could consistently meditate on Peace with the thumb and index fingers, Listening to the Answers, for the thumb and middle fingers, and so on.

Example

Clint is just about to go home to his daughter's birthday party when his Boss comes into his office, needing "Just one more thing..."

Clint regularly practices meditating using the ring finger knotting technique, and so discretely interlinks the rings of his index fingers and thumbs beneath the desk and out of his Boss's sight. He feels a wave of peace wash over him and calmly replies

"Can it wait to tomorrow? I have to get to my daughter's birthday party."

Whatever happens next will probably go better than if Clint had gone down the path of aldrenalin and cortisol, reacted angrily, either snapping at his boss, or begrudgingly doing it and then arriving home in a foul mood for the end of his daughter's birthday.

Kata

"It's a lot like dancing" ~ *Terry Dobson*

In Japanese martial arts, Kata are pre-arranged

sequences of moves that often look a lot like dancing. They're usually designed for one or two people. Line dancing is a good example of this. And of course, there's nothing stopping you learning a martial arts kata and doing it to either music or silence as a form of meditation. (Most eastern martial arts have a version of kata, but the name varies, such as "form" or "pattern.") Each day in China, parks are filled with people quietly going through Tai Chi forms.

To meditate, get changed into whatever clothing or shoes you need. Chose the rhythm and movements you want to use.

Bring your focus to what you want to meditate on.

Start to repeat the rhythm(s) and movements over and over. Let it bring you into a meditative state.

Example

Jeff is trying to decide whether or not to take a job offer. He fixes his intention on Listening to the Answers and begins "Walking the Circle" from Bagwa. The form is familiar to him and he lets it center him, gradually clearing away the noise and chatter in his mind. Slowly his mind begins to calm and clear, like a pond returning to a pristine state after a pebble has been thrown into it, as he reaches a state of Mushin.

He continues to "Walk the circle", focusing on his intention and remaining centered, without forcing anything, until a thought pops into his head reminding him of a friend who used to be in this field and could give better insights into the decision.

He calmly stops, takes a moment and then reaches for his phone to call them.

Showers

"Why do answers always come to me in the shower?" - *Albert Einstein*

Particularly if shampoo and conditioner are involved, showers usually require a certain amount of killing time.

Which is a wasted opportunity.

The droplets of water fall on you rhythmically, making it easier to enter a meditative state. This was why Einstein kept getting his answers – his mind shifted into a theta state, allowing his unconscious some space to let the answers come to the surface.

Example

Stacy steps into her shower and chooses her intention as Listening to the Answers. At first, she brings her focus to the drops of water falling onto her skin. She lets her mind empty and center, until she reaches a state of Mushin and listens.

Chakras

We tend to associate certain feelings with certain parts of our body. When we're injured, we instinctively reach to touch the pain with our hands. We experience nervous butterflies in our stomach, and do our thinking in our head.

Chakras are a way of bringing this together.

For meditation, you can use chakras in a similar manner to the 'rings' in finger knotting. Only instead of knotting your fingers, you focus on the area of your body that corresponds to a specific chakra. You may find you like to rest your hands gently on it.

For some, assigning colors or sounds to each chakra helps as well. A lot of material has been written on this subject, far too much to cover here, but a simple internet search, or trip to your library or bookstore, will give you more information on colors etc, if you're interested.

For the purposes of this book, the crown of your head is often associated with a connection to the Divine. The heart is associated with love and wishing well to others, and so combines well with the Meditation of Loving Kindness.

The "third eye", situated between and slightly above the eyebrows is associated with Listening to the Answers.

All three work well for meditating on Peace.

Example

Helen arrives home after a long day at work. She

retreats to her bedroom, changes into more comfortable clothes and lies down on her bed. She places the palms of her hands over her heart, closes her eyes and begins the Meditation of Loving Kindness, focusing her intention on the Divine with the abstract idea of Love.

When she finishes, she settles down for a refreshing nap.

Incense

Incense utilizes something that tends to be overlooked - our sense of smell. Smell is an incredibly powerful way of anchoring. The scent of cotton candy can take us back to summer vacations as a child.

There are many objects you can use when meditating with incense.

First, you need to choose what you want to burn? Fortunately, there's no need to re-invent the wheel; incense is readily available as oil, sticks, "tears" (incense in pellet-form), or smudge sticks.

Then you need to decide on the object in which the incense is going to burn.

Sticks ideally need a holder. Oil or tears can be placed in a burner, of which there are a number of varieties;

possibly the most interesting of which is called a "waterfall burner" which creates the illusion of a waterfall with the incense's smoke. Smudge sticks are essentially feathers with incense that you wave around the room.

Lastly, how are you going to light and extinguish it? Matches and cigarette lighters are the most common solution.

As always with meditation, find what appeals most to you. If you wish, an internet search of "incense types", or trip to your local library or bookstore will give you information on what the different incenses are traditionally used for, though the much of this information is based on magick. Generally speaking, have a look on bubble bath to see what refreshes, calms and so on. For example, lavender, sandalwood and vanilla all have a calming effect.

An option with anchoring is to use one type of incense for each intention, eg sandalwood for Peace frankincense for Listening to the Answers and sage for the Divine.

Trouble-shooting

There are a few extra considerations when using incense. Make sure the room is well ventilated so the smoke can safely disperse and doesn't hinder the breathing of anyone there. If you, or anyone else who's going to enter the room, suffer from asthma or similar respiratory issues, consult a doctor first.

If you use matches, have something non-flammable like a ceramic dish to put them in after you've extinguished them. If you're using a holder, make sure it's secure and choose a place where it isn't close to any flammable materials, in case it falls over.

And lastly, don't try to extinguish oil with water. It will go everywhere and stay alight! (A friend once napalmed her desk when she tried this.)

For a safer version, scented bubble bath has much the same effect, as does placing a little scented massage oil on your neck, though don't fall asleep in the bath and be careful not to get oil on your clothes! You'll probably want some tissues or a cloth nearby to clean your hands too.

Example

Mike has had enough of Christmas rush-hour traffic. He's already had three near collisions, two of whom were with drivers on their phones! He feels the cortisol and aldrenalin flowing through him and decides getting home late is better than ending up in A&E; so he pulls over and gets out a bottle of lavender massage oil from his glove compartment.

He unwraps it from an old handkerchief and gently applies a drop to each side of his neck, massaging it into his skin with small circular motions with his fingertips, before wiping them clean on the handkerchief. He reclines the car chair so it's more comfortable, closes his eyes and focuses his intention on Peace.

As he breathes, he enjoys the calming effect of the Lavender and feels himself centering; dopamine kicks in from enjoying the lavender and knowing he's in his own space, counter-acting and lower the effects of the cortisol and aldrenalin.

Summary

- Focusing on the physicality of these meditations and the feelings they invoke, has a strong anchoring effect.

- 3 Breaths: Something positive and abstract, something you find awe-inspiring, settle and center yourself.

- It's ok to build up to three whole breaths and they don't need to be the same length.

- Use something you think about a lot to remind you to do this first.

- Children's games are often meditations in disguise, but using "having fun" as the intention.

- Strings of beads are a simple way to keep track of where you are in a meditation without needed to look. They also can be worn as jewelry, and used discretely.

- Finger knotting can also be done discretely, especially making finger rings.

- You can anchor different intentions to different fingers.

- Kata are sets of movements. Chose one to

meditate with, adjusting the length and complexity to suit you.

- The rhythmic nature of showers helps shift you into a meditative theta state, especially that associated with Listening to the Answers.

- Chakras are an effective way of anchoring parts of your body to specific emotions and meditative states.

- Smell has a powerful anchoring effect, making Incense very effective for meditating. Just be careful of the fire hazards.

Chapter 7 Combinations

"The mind can go in a thousand directions, but on this

beautiful path, I walk in peace.

With each step, the wind blows.

With each step, a flower blooms."

~ Thich Nhat Hanh

There are also some forms of meditation which combine more two or more of Seeing, Hearing, Feeling and Doing. Looking out over the ocean, you can see the sunlight dancing on the waves, listen as they crash against the shore and feel the salty spray against your skin.

You may find you're someone who finds certain combinations to be more pleasing and effective for your meditation. As always, try them out and discover which you find work best and fit into your life. Ultimately, all these forms of meditation are just different ways of climbing up the same mountain.

Drumming

Drumming has been used in meditation forever. Our minds respond strongly to rhythms and drums are one of the purest ways of sounding a rhythm.

Probably the biggest issue with producing drumming yourself is annoying your neighbors! Even its "little sister" version of tapping will quickly annoy those around you, especially if you do it at work!

One solution is to drum or tap on the areas of your body that have large muscles — such as your arms or legs. This deadens the sounds, but you'll still be able to feel the beats. Drumming is so powerful, that even seeing someone doing this can be distracting; in which case, simply tap or drum on your thighs while sitting at a desk to hide it from view.

Drumming is unusual in that you can use it to both increase or decrease the amount of aldrenalin in your body, depending on how fast you go. Calm, soothing beats with lower it, whilst something a bit more like Animal from the Muppets will raise it. What's particularly useful is that you get to experience aldrenalin without cortisol — something that's increasingly rare in modern society.

To meditate, first get whatever you need for your

drumming prepared. Chose the rhythm(s) you want to use.

Bring your focus to what you want to meditate on.

Start to repeat the rhythm(s) over and over. Let it bring you into a meditative state.

Example

Chloe spent six months searching thrift stores and the internet until she finally found a drum that suited her. It was old, battered and clearly well-used, but in a loved kind of way, rather than in a "used once and left in the attic for years" vibe.

Each morning, she carefully stows it in her backpack and cycles to the top of a nearby hill, arriving just before dawn. It's always deserted then. Her friend Sue arrives at about the same time, with her own drum. They great each other with a hug, enjoying the oxytocin it creates.

They bring their focus to the Divine and reverently unpack their drums, sitting down in the same spot they always do, each with their drum in front of them. Chloe begins to beat out a simple rhythm, letting it hold her intention as she looks out over the landscape below and marvels at the beauty of Nature.

Sue joins in, layering different rhythms over the top of

it.

They don't keep track of time, simply staying as long as feels right, before finally ending their drumming, enjoying the mix of aldrenalin, oxytocin and dopamine, before taking one last look around and then calmly packing up and cycling home once more.

Crystals

Crystals can be used for meditating in a number of ways. Ideally, if you find a shop that sells them, you can pick up different crystals and gemstones. Have a play with them to discover what appeals to you. What size and weight do you prefer? Which colors and textures? Do you like how do they interact with light?

Or if you want, there's a lot of information written in books and internet on the associated properties of various gems eg snowflake obsidian - pictured above - is associated with finding balance. A google search for "Gemstone properties" will get you started if that interests you.

Once you've got them, you can carry them around in a drawstring bag. As always, feel free to search around until you find one that really appeals to you.

To meditate, pull them out during the day and just enjoy holding them, or play with moving them around in your hand. You can also create patterns with them. Depending on their size and shape, you may be able to stack them to a certain degree.

Enjoy the sense of wonder.

Crystals are excellent for anchoring. You can associate specific crystals with focusing your awareness in specific ways, eg Peace. You can also anchor specific patterns to individual focuses, similar to creating your own mandala.

Example

Clive finds a "New Age" shop that sells gemstones. He

looks at the various trays of them and picks out three that he just really likes, knowing that will give him a boost in dopamine when he uses them. He then chooses an intention for each.

He then spends five minutes each day holding one of the stones and meditating on the intention he chose for it. As months pass, he finds as soon as he holds a stone, he starts shifting into the meditative state he anchored to it.

Mixing them together

You can also combine different meditations into one. A lot of religious ceremonies do this: candles, incense, music, mantras and so on, all at once.

Example

Mike is still relaxing in his car, enjoying the scented oil and waiting for the Christmas traffic to subside. He turns on the car stereo and listens to soothing music as he meditates on Peace.

Summary

🌀 There are also some forms of meditation which combine more two or more of Seeing, Hearing, Feeling and Doing.

🌀 You can expand the Flowing Water meditation to include Listening to the sound it makes, as well as how it looks.

🌀 Drumming combines Listening with Feeling and Doing. You can do it more discretely by tapping your body.

🌀 Crystals combine Seeing with Feeling and Doing. You can anchor different intentions to different crystals.

🌀 You can also combine different meditations to make new ones.

Chapter 8 Now It's Your Turn

"A journey of ten thousand miles begins with a single step." ~ *Lao Tzu*

By now you've seen a good range of ways to meditate. You can choose from these, or use them to inspire you to try others. There's just one more crucial element.

You have to start.

The above off-quoted phrase by Lao Tzu seems simple enough – for now, just deal with beginning, don't worry about the rest of the journey.

But it has some helpful extra meanings hidden within. When it was first written down, there was no word for "infinity." Instead, "ten thousand" was used as code to mean "infinite", or "beyond comprehension".

Imagine a pink elephant – pretty easy. Now try two, then ten, then a thousand! Suddenly all the detail has vanished into a sea of pink. There comes a point where although we intellectually understand what large numbers mean, we can't mentally cope with them without somehow making them smaller. It's easy to visualize a hundred dollar bill, but It's impossible to visualize a hundred, separate dollar bills.

In the same way, the more detail we try to imagine in the journey ahead, the more overwhelmed we become, defeating ourselves before we've even put a single step on the path.

The other hidden Easter egg in this quote is Lao Tzu 'himself.'

A group of wise, elderly men had finally had enough of where they lived and were leaving never to return. The guard at the gate, realizing the mess the town was going to descend into, refused to let them leave until they had written down their best advice. "Lao Tzu" literally just means "old man."

Fortunately, the old men lived up to their reputation and gave some good advice. In this case, the most important thing about meditating is to start. It doesn't matter if it's the basic meditation at the beginning of this book where you just think about peace for a moment, or something more elaborate.

Take the first step.

Making it your own

Now that you have a clearer idea of the basic structure, it's time to start filling it in. If you're still not sure about some parts, just try different answers until you find what fits for you.

Decide if you want to have:

A specific time set aside for meditating. When and for how long?

A specific place. If so, are you going to enter and exit it in a particular way? Are you going to wear specific clothing, or sit in a certain way?

Are you going to do this alone or with others in the same place?

If with others, are they going to join in? Are they going to be aware of what you're doing?

Specific objects. If so, are you going to take them out and put them away in a certain fashion?

Choose your intention.

Choose how you want to meditate.

Meditate.

End your meditation in the way you have chosen.

Bringing meditation into your everyday life

"Time is too slow for those who wait, too swift for those who fear, too long for those who grieve, too short for those who rejoice, but for those who love, time is eternity." – Henry Van Dyke.

Let's revisit Nick and see how the same day could have gone if he knew how to meditate.

Nick wakes up to his alarm clock. But this time, he pauses and takes a deep breath to center himself. Getting comfortable lying on his back and keeping his eyes closed, he brings his intention to Peace.

Nick begins using the mala on his wrist. He knows how many times he needs to go completely around it, taking one breath for each bead, for five minutes to pass, so he doesn't need to keep checking the clock or set another alarm.

At the end of five minutes, he calmly gets up and dressed according to his own ritual. Left sock on first, and so on, each completed part giving him some dopamine. After eating breakfast he walks to the bus stop. As he waits for the bus (which is going to be late!) he moves his intention to the Divine and uses the Meditation of Loving

Kindness. The bus finally arrives and everyone surges forwards, each convinced that their need to be on time is the most important.

Nick manages to squeeze on and spends the journey meditating on Listening to the Answers by focusing on his breathing. As it centers him to Mushin, insights gradually start to trickle into his mind on ways of approaching the day ahead at work, giving him small boosts of dopamine. He gets off the bus without any cortisol or aldrenalin rushing through him.

He finally arrives at his office, slightly late, and gets a disapproving look from his boss. He takes a moment to bringing his intention to the Divine, with a micro-version of the Meditation of Loving Kindness that lasts for three breaths, stopping the coritsol and aldrenalin before they get any momentum.

He grabs two cups of coffee and heads over to his boss. Giving his boss one of the coffees, Nick apologizes for being late, explaining that New York traffic was to blame. As his boss takes the coffee, they both get a boost of oxytocin, helping them to see each other as comrades, rather than adversaries. Nick then asks for feedback on one of the ideas that occurred to him while on the bus about an effective way of dealing with a problematic client.

The day continues with fresh mayhem; people wanting things done with no notice and little explanation. Nick periodically takes brief moments to catch his breath and meditate on Peace, Listening to the Answers, or Love, depending on which seems most useful at the time; sometimes discretely using his mala under the desk. This helps him keep his aldrenalin and cortisol in check, while boosting his oxytocin and dopamine.

He gets lunch and then takes it outside to eat, recognizing that he'll be more productive if he takes some time now to rest and re-charge. He meditates on the Divine - the beauty that surrounds him and the amazing feats of human engineering that create and maintain the city around him. This further helps him reset from any remaining aldrenalin and cortisol, while boosting his dopamine.

Finally, the work-day comes to an end. He still leaves half an hour late, but uses the journey home to center himself and meditate on Peace. While the people around him are drunk on frustration, and worn down by their cortisol and aldrenalin, Nick is largely unaffected.

When he finally gets home, he goes through another ritual of getting changed, showering and preparing his meal. He then settles down to watch tv shows.

He goes through another ritual of getting washed and changed for bed. He spends five minutes lying on his back, first getting comfortable and then meditating on Peace as he breathes.

Nick falls asleep to peaceful dreams.

~

Meditation didn't "fix" Nick's day. The bus was still late, the boss was annoyed, ungrateful people gave him too much to do and he was surrounded by frustrated, busy people from the moment he left home. Nor did it take up any real time. At no point did he meditate on a mountain for an hour – that was never going to fit into the time he had available.

What changed was how he reacted to what was happening. By meditating, even in tiny amounts, he was better able to stay calm and find the eye of the storm, rather than getting emotionally tossed around.

However, in all likelihood, Nick's day would have been better. Being centered and wishing well to those around you, tends to bring out the better side in people. Sure, some lunatics will still cut you up in traffic and then swear at you.

But it's surprising how far a little kindness can go.

Summary

● Take the first step. Good luck!

Made in the USA
Monee, IL
05 December 2020

51112916R00075